Lunchbox Words

Lunchbox
Words

Text by **Tracey West**

Art by **James K. Hindle**

Roaring Brook Press
New York

Text copyright © 2017 by Roaring Brook Press
Illustrations copyright © 2017 by Roaring Brook Press
Published by Roaring Brook Press

Roaring Brook Press is a division of
Holtzbrinck Publishing Holdings Limited Partnership
175 Fifth Avenue, New York, NY 10010

mackids.com

Library of Congress Cataloging-in-Publication Data
Names: West, Tracey, 1965– author. | Hindle, James K., illustrator.
Title: Lunchbox words : 65 word-based notes to pack in your speller's lunchbox or
     backpack / text by Tracey West ; illustrations by James K.
     Hindle.
Description: First edition. | New York : Roaring Brook Press, 2017. | Series:
     Scripps National Spelling Bee
Identifiers: LCCN 2016047516 | ISBN 9781626727182 (pbk.) | ISBN 9781626721746
     (hardcover)
Subjects: LCSH: English language—Orthography and spelling—Study and
     teaching—United States. | English language—Orthography and spelling—
     Study and teaching—Juvenile literature. | Education—Parental participation.
Classification: LCC PE1145.2 .W44 2016 | DDC 421.54—dc23
LC record available at https://lccn.loc.gov/2016047516

Our books may be purchased in bulk for promotional, educational, or business
use. Please contact your local bookseller or the Macmillan Corporate and
Premium Sales Department at (800) 221-7945 ext. 5442 or by e-mail at
MacmillanSpecialMarkets@macmillan.com.

First edition, 2017
Book design by Roberta Pressel
Printed in the United States of America by LSC Communications, Harrisonburg,
Virginia

10 9 8 7 6 5 4 3 2 1

INTRODUCTION

Helping kids learn the words they need for success in life is my main job as executive director of the Scripps National Spelling Bee. Through development of quality educational materials and high-profile contests, my colleagues and I work diligently to put the spotlight on words that will become difference-makers for kids. It's gratifying to see kids in spelling bees light up with smiles when they are asked to spell words they know. The inspiration for our efforts, however, is imagining all the smiles that come long afterward when they:

- feel familiar with many of the vocabulary terms in their high school and college classes;

- confidently deliver a presentation before an audience because they're already experienced in performing in front of others;

- comprehend challenging reading sections in college-entry examinations;

- secure the jobs of their dreams because they used English well in their interviews, and because their résumés were free of spelling and grammar errors; and, eventually,

- answer the many "What does it mean?" and "How do you say this?" questions from their own children.

Giving kids the words they need is more than a professional endeavor. It's personal, and that's because I'm a mom.

When my son was in the early elementary grades, I wanted to write sweet notes of encouragement and slip them into his packed lunches. The truth is that it never happened. Working-mom life got in the way. By the time he was a fourth grader, I knew that the notes-in-his-lunchbox idea would cause embarrassment, so I resolved to slip notes into his backpack. Again, working-mom life got in the way.

So before he departed for his first weeklong summer camp experience, I sneaked into his already-packed suitcase. Carefully and quickly lifting out shoes, a towel, socks, and shirts, I found what I was looking for at the bottom—six pairs of athletic shorts. Into the pockets of the shorts I slipped notes, each with an inspirational quote, advice, or silly saying:

KEEP CALM AND CAMP ON.
♥ MOM

"A PERSON WHO NEVER MADE A MISTAKE NEVER TRIED
ANYTHING NEW." —ALBERT EINSTEIN
♥ MOM

BE THE REASON SOMEONE SMILES TODAY.
♥ MOM

In that moment, I was temporarily liberated from Mom Guilt—the guilt that comes from being too busy to make Pinterest-worthy healthy and delicious packed lunches, beautiful scrapbooks documenting every vacation and milestone, and designer tween bedrooms worthy of an HGTV show.

Summer camp came and went, and my son said nothing about what he found in his pockets. Finally, I asked him about it. The blush and sheepish sweet grin that followed let me know all I needed: he liked the notes! In that moment I realized kids appreciate what we as moms do without ever finding the words *thank you*, and that's okay. The thank-you will come in the years ahead.

I also realized I could have earned that sheepish sweet grin for notewriting years ago if only I had a little help. That's where this book comes into the picture. Let the notes here inspire you to write your own, or tear out a page to tuck into a lunchbox or backpack. Remember that it's those special "Love, Mom" touches that really make the gesture resonate.

Your child will learn and smile, and you'll feel like the mom of your dreams.

Paige Kimble

PAIGE KIMBLE

Mom of Two
Executive Director of the Scripps National Spelling Bee
1981 Scripps National Spelling Bee Champion

DELICIOUS

word	delicious
pronunciation	dee-LISH-us
part of speech	adjective
definition	very good to taste

Delicious is an adjective that describes something that tastes very good. *Yummy* and *tasty* are other words that mean the same thing as *delicious*.

The word *delicious* doesn't follow normal spelling rules. The *c* in the word is pronounced to make a "sh" sound—"dee-LISH-us." How can you remember the *c* in *delicious*? Just remember that when you "c" something delicious, you want to eat it!

What kind of fruit do ghosts think is the most delicious? *Boo*-berries!

TEAMWORK

is a great way to solve
problems.
Ask a friend
if you need
help!

TEAMWORK

word	teamwork
pronunciation	TEEM-wurk
part of speech	noun
definition	work done together

Teamwork is a noun that means "work that people do together—as a team!" You can use teamwork to bake a cake or to build a house.

   Teamwork is spelled as one word. To remember this, just think: *Team* and *work* work together to make one word!

What kind of work can never be done alone?
Teamwork!

I know you'll
do great work today
because
I BELIEVE
in you. I hope you
BELIEVE in
yourself, too.

BELIEVE

word	believe
pronunciation	be-LEEV
part of speech	verb
definition	to accept as true

When you believe in something, you think it is true. If people say they believe in you, it means they think you will succeed.

To remember that there is an *i* in the word *believe*, try thinking of this sentence: I believe there is an *i* in *believe*.

> **"I do believe in fairies!"**
> —*Peter Pan*, the musical

Be
GENEROUS
with your smiles,
and you'll get
some in return.

GENEROUS

word   generous

pronunciation   JEN-ur-us

part of speech   adjective

definition   very giving of kindness, time, or money

A generous person is someone who is very giving of kindness, time, or money.

The word *generous* begins with a *g* that is pronounced like a *j*. To remember that *generous* begins with a *g*, try thinking of these things that people can be generous with: gifts, goodies, and grins. They all begin with the letter *g*, too!

Which animal is the most generous?
A hermit crab—he'll give you the shell off his back!

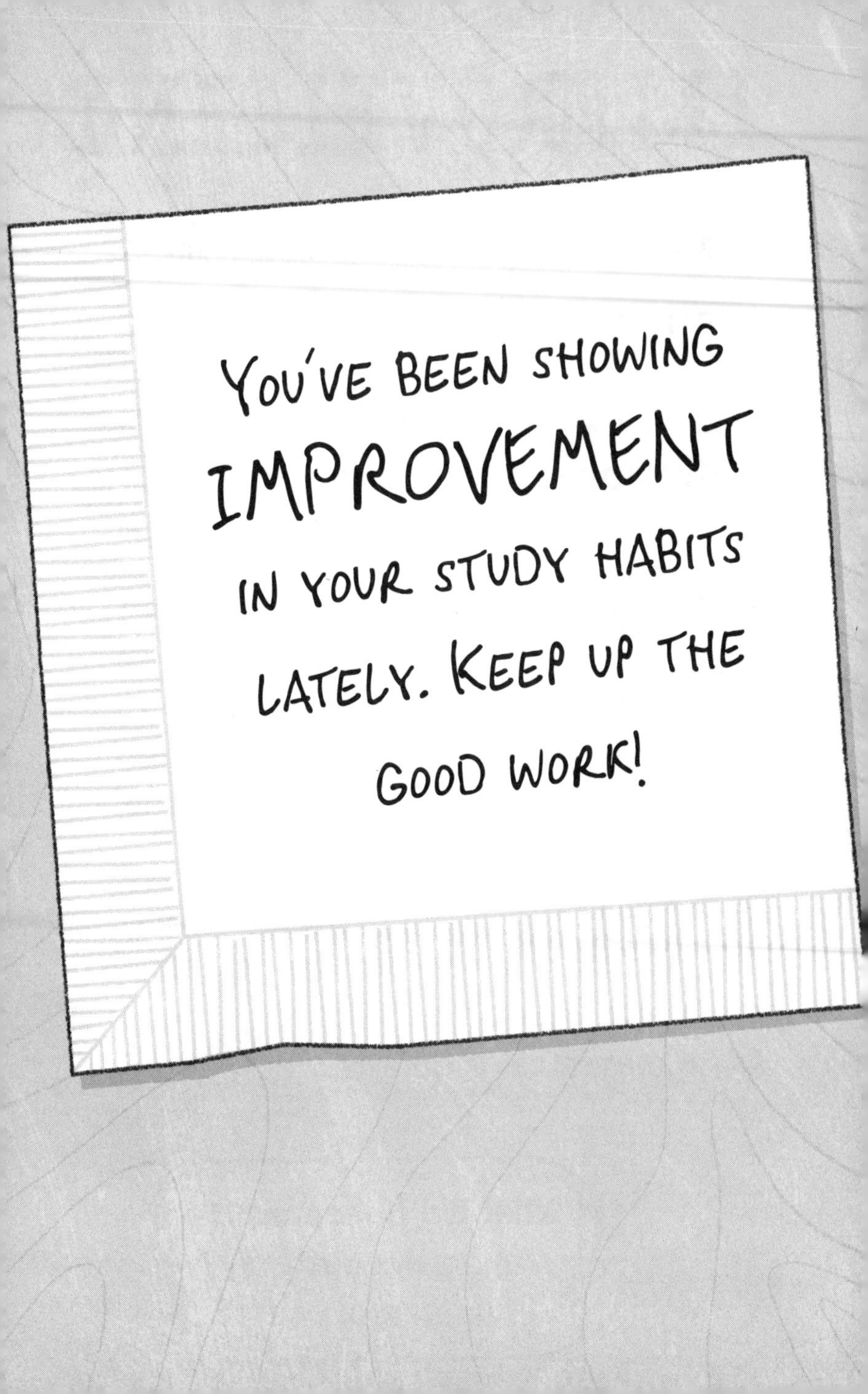
You've been showing IMPROVEMENT in your study habits lately. Keep up the good work!

IMPROVEMENT

word　　　　　　　improvement

pronunciation　　im-PROOV-munt

part of speech　　noun

definition　　　　the action of making
something better

An improvement is an action that makes something better.

The word is made up of two parts: *improve* + *ment*. The M-E-N-T combination at the end of the word *improvement* indicates that it is a noun. You might be tempted to spell the word with an *a* or a *u* instead of an *e* because of how it sounds: "im-PROOV-munt." Use this sentence to remember the M-E combination in *improvement*: An improvement can improve me.

What did the caterpillar say to the butterfly?
Nice improvement!

Here's a tip to help you EXCEL on your test: Read each question carefully before you answer.

EXCEL

word excel

pronunciation ek-SEL

part of speech verb

definition to do very well

Excel is a verb that means "to do very well." You can excel at doing lots of things, like playing a sport or an instrument.

 Excel is pronounced "ek-SEL," but there is no *s* in the word. The "s" sound is made by the letter *c*.

Why did the pig excel at acting? Because she was a real ham!

I CAN'T WAIT
TO HEAR ALL THE
NEW AND
WONDERFUL
THINGS YOU
LEARNED IN SCHOOL
TODAY!

WONDERFUL

word	wonderful
pronunciation	WUN-dur-ful
part of speech	adjective
definition	very good

Wonderful is an adjective that means "very good." When you see something very good, it fills you with wonder.

Because *wonderful* ends with the sound "ful," it is tempting to put an extra *l* on the end, as in *full*. Just remember: You only need one *l* to be wonderful!

Which animals make the most wonderful teachers?
Fish, because they spend all their time in schools!

Every day brings
an OPPORTUNITY
to make a friend.
Say hi to
someone new.

OPPORTUNITY

word	opportunity
pronunciation	ah-pur-TOO-nuh-tee
part of speech	noun
definition	a chance to do something

An opportunity is a chance to do something. If someone gives you tickets to a show, you will have an opportunity to see that show.

Opportunity has five syllables. When spelling the word, say each syllable to yourself slowly to sound it out: op-por-tu-ni-ty.

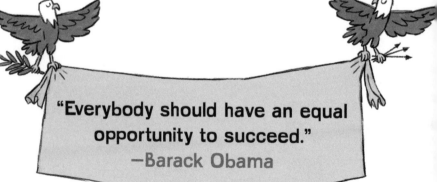

"**Everybody should have an equal opportunity to succeed.**"
—Barack Obama

Did you know that the turkey sandwich is the number-one favorite sandwich in the United States? What kind of sandwich do you ENJOY most?

ENJOY

word	enjoy
pronunciation	en-JOY
part of speech	verb
definition	to take delight in something

Enjoy is a verb that means "to take delight in something." When you enjoy something, it makes you happy.

It might be tempting to spell the word with an *i* as the first letter. Try to remember that *enjoy* starts with an *e*, because things you *en*joy are *e*xcellent!

What breakfast cereal do cats enjoy most?
Mice Crispies!

UNIQUE

word — unique

pronunciation — yoo-NEEK

part of speech — adjective

definition — special and unlike anything else

Unique is an adjective that describes something that is not like anything else; something unique is one of a kind. The first part of the word, *uni*, means "one." Think of a *uni*corn, with its one horn.

The word *unique* is pronounced "yoo-NEEK." The letter combination Q-U-E makes the "k" sound in the word.

"The more you are like yourself, the less you are like anyone else, which makes you unique."
—Walt Disney

What
DISCOVERY
will you make today?
Tonight, ask yourself
what you found out
today that you didn't
know this morning.

DISCOVERY

word   discovery

pronunciation   dis-KUH-vuh-ree

part of speech   noun

definition   the act of learning
                            or finding something
                            that had been unknown

When you make a discovery, you learn or find
something that you didn't know before. Finding a
dinosaur bone in your yard would be a big discovery.
Learning the meaning of a new word is a discovery,
too!

The *y* at the end of *discovery* sounds
like an "e."

**How did Ben Franklin
feel after his discovery
of electricity?**
Shocked!

It's okay to
DAYDREAM
once in a while,
but make sure
you don't fall
asleep!

DAYDREAM

word   daydream

pronunciation   DAY-dreem

part of speech   verb

definition   to think pleasant thoughts that distract you from what is actually happening

When you daydream, you use your imagination to think nice thoughts that distract you from what is really happening.

Daydream is one word made up of two different words: *day* + *dream*.

> **"You get ideas from daydreaming."**
> —Neil Gaiman

If you do your very best, you can always hold your head up PROUDLY.

PROUDLY

word	proudly
pronunciation	PROWD-lee
part of speech	adverb
definition	in a manner pleased with oneself or someone else due to an accomplishment or characteristic

To do something proudly means to do it with pride—a sense of accomplishment. You can proudly march in a parade or proudly cross the finish line at the end of a race. What else can you do proudly?

Proudly is an adverb—a word that describes an action. When a word ends in the letters *-ly*, it is a clue that it might be an adverb, describing how something is done.

"O say can you see,
by the dawn's early light,
what so proudly we hailed
at the twilight's last gleaming."
—*The Star-Spangled Banner*

I can't wait to have a SPIRITED conversation with you about everything you did at school today!

SPIRITED

word	spirited
pronunciation	SPIR-it-id
part of speech	adjective
definition	lively and full of energy

The word *spirit* means "energy." School spirit is a feeling of positive energy about your school. So when something is *spirited*, it means it is full of energy.

To remember how to spell the *spirit* part of *spirited*, think of a spirited cheerleader leading this cheer: S-P-I, R-I-T! Spirit leads to vic-to-ry!

Whom should you invite to your party to make sure it is spirited? A ghost, of course!

CREATIVITY ISN'T JUST FOR ART CLASS. USING YOUR IMAGINATION CAN HELP YOU IN ALL OF YOUR SUBJECTS.

CREATIVITY

word	creativity
pronunciation	kree-ay-TIV-uh-tee
part of speech	noun
definition	the quality of using your imagination and having original ideas

The word *creativity* is made up of: *creative + ity*. To spell *creativity*, remember to drop the *e* before adding the *-ity*.

Creativity is the act of using your imagination and having new ideas. *Creative* is an adjective, but the word becomes a noun when you add the ending *-ity*.

"Creativity is intelligence having fun."
—Albert Einstein

If someone
offers help,
ACCEPT it!
Next time, it may
be your turn to help
someone else.

ACCEPT

word	accept
pronunciation	ak-SEPT
part of speech	verb
definition	to receive

When you accept something, you receive it or get it. You can accept an apple from a friend, or you can accept an award from an organization.

It is easy to mix up *accept* with the word *except*, since they sound so similar. *Except* means "not including." Here's a trick to remember that *accept* means "to receive." Memorize this sentence: Always accept apples. *Always*, *accept*, and *apples* all begin with the letter *a*.

"I can accept failure. Everyone fails at something. But I cannot accept not trying."
—Michael Jordan

FORTUNATELY

FOR YOU, I
REMEMBERED TO
INCLUDE YOUR
FAVORITE SNACK.
I HOPE IT'S A BRIGHT
SPOT IN YOUR DAY!

FORTUNATELY

word	fortunately
pronunciation	FOHR-chuh-nit-lee
part of speech	adverb
definition	to do with or due to good luck

Fortunately means "to do something by good luck."

    Fortunately is made up of two parts: *fortunate* + *ly*. The *-ly* ending tells you that the word is an adverb. When you spell *fortunately*, do not drop the *e* when you add the *-ly*. Remember: The *e* in *fortunately* is lucky because it gets to stay in the word!

Did you hear about the elephant who had to take a last-minute trip? Fortunately, he always had his trunk with him.

If you can,
do something
HELPFUL
for a teacher
today.

HELPFUL

word	helpful
pronunciation	HELP-ful
part of speech	adjective
definition	ready or willing to assist

A person who is helpful is ready or willing to assist.

Helpful is made up of two parts: *help* + *ful*. The *-ful* ending tells you that the word is an adjective. You might be tempted to put an extra *l* on the end of the word, like the word *full*. But remember that *helpful*, like other adjectives, has only one *l* on the end.

Why aren't snakes helpful?
Because they can never give you a hand!

Here's a math test tip: After you find the SOLUTION to a problem, do the problem a second time to make sure you get the same result.

SOLUTION

word	solution
pronunciation	suh-LOO-shun
part of speech	noun
definition	the answer to a problem

Solution is a noun that means "the answer to a problem."

The word is pronounced "suh-LOO-shun," and the T-I-O-N combination makes the "shun" sound at the end. You can remember this by thinking of other words that end in T-I-O-N: To get the solu*tion*, you will need all the informa*tion*.

What's the best solution for a gorilla with a broken bike?
Give her a monkey wrench so she can fix it!

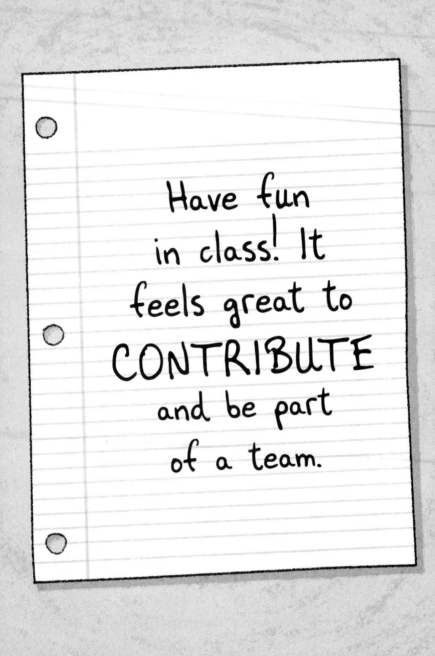

CONTRIBUTE

word   contribute

pronunciation   kun-TRIB-yoot

part of speech   verb

definition   to add ideas, effort, or support to a project or activity

When you contribute to something, you add to it. You can contribute your talent to a show, your ideas to a project, or your money to a cause, to name just a few things.

Contribute has a silent *e* on the end of the word. That *e* helps give the *u* its "ew" sound. So the silent *e* contributes to the word!

"I think we need more love in the world . . . I definitely want to contribute to that."
—Ellen DeGeneres

Do your best every time, and you'll be CONTENT when your work is finished.

CONTENT

word	content
pronunciation	kun-TENT
part of speech	adjective
definition	pleased, with no reason to complain

When the word *content* is an adjective, it describes the feeling of being pleased or happy. *Content* is an adjective when emphasis is placed on the word's second syllable: "kun-TENT."

The word *content* can also be a noun when it is pronounced with emphasis placed on the first syllable: "KON-tent." Then it means "something that is held inside something else." For example, you can feel con*tent* about the *con*tent in a book.

Why are fish content to live in salt water? Because pepper makes them sneeze!

You have
CONSISTENTLY
been doing your
very best work.
Keep it up!

CONSISTENTLY

word	consistently
pronunciation	kun-SIS-tent-lee
part of speech	adverb
definition	in a manner that is even, regular, or not changing

When you do something consistently, you do it the same way every time. *Consistently* is an adverb because it describes *how* you do something. The *-ly* ending is another clue that the word is an adverb.

There are four syllables in this word: con-sis-tent-ly. This word is easier to spell if you spell it out slowly, one syllable at a time!

Why are frogs consistently happy? Because they eat what bugs them!

Act with
GRACE
when things get
tough. You'll
be proud of
yourself!

GRACE

word	grace
pronunciation	grays
part of speech	noun
definition	smoothness or elegance in movement or manners

When you move your body with grace or behave with grace, it means you do those things smoothly. You can sway and step with grace when you dance. And if a friend makes you mad and you keep your cool, you are acting with grace.

The letter *c* in *grace* sounds like an "s" in the word. The following sentence has other words that end with A-C-E: She ran with grace in the race and finished in first place.

Why can't four-legged animals dance with grace? Because they've got two left feet!

Eating
a good lunch is
IMPORTANT.
Food is fuel for
your brain!

IMPORTANT

word	important
pronunciation	im-POHR-tunt
part of speech	adjective
definition	very significant or valuable

When something is important, it means a lot to you or is worth a lot. Other words that mean the same thing as *important* are *main* and *major*.

Important ends in the letters A-N-T. To help you remember these letters, think of how busy a worker ant can be when it gathers food. That is one important ant!

> **"The most important thing is to inspire people so they can be great in whatever they want to do."**
> **—Kobe Bryant**

When things get tough, remember that every day of school gets you one step closer to a brighter FUTURE.

FUTURE

word   future

pronunciation FYOO-chur

part of speech noun

definition   the time following
         the current time

The word *future* means "the time following the
time it is now." So the future can be just one
second from now or a million years from now!

 Future is pronounced "FYOO-chur." The *t* in
future makes the "ch" sound. Just remember:
There's no *ch* in *future*!

**Why did the students all
fall asleep in class?**
Because their teacher
told them to dream
about the future!

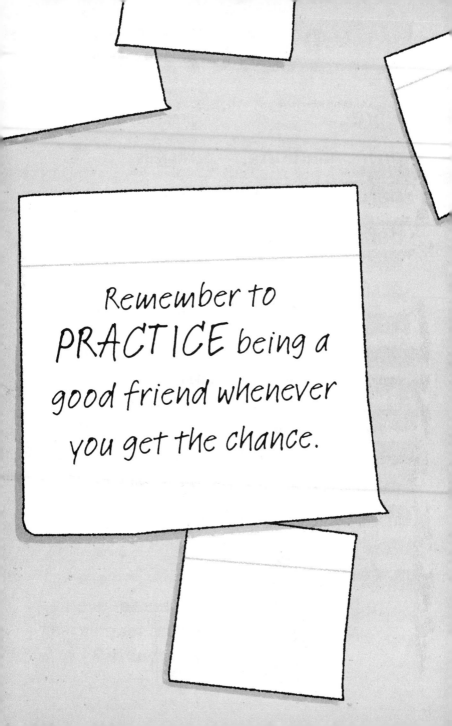

PRACTICE

word   practice

pronunciation   PRAK-tis

part of speech verb

definition   to repeatedly exercise
a skill, activity, or
performance in
order to improve

When you practice something, you do it again and
again to get better at it. You can practice playing
baseball or practice being a better friend.

 The word *practice* is pronounced "PRAK-tis." The
letter combination I-C-E sounds like "iss." How can
you remember that *practice* ends in *-ice*? Think
about this: Ice skaters practice a lot!

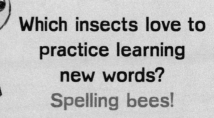

**Which insects love to
practice learning
new words?**
Spelling bees!

When you approach things with a POSITIVE outlook, you're bound to get POSITIVE results!

POSITIVE

word   positive

pronunciation   PAHZ-uh-tiv

part of speech   adjective

definition   showing confidence

When you feel positive about something, you feel good about it and confident that it will turn out all right. Because *positive* is a word that describes a feeling, a thought, or another noun, it's an adjective.

Positive is made up of three syllables: pos-i-tive. It might be tempting to put an *a* in the middle of the word instead of an *i*. When you spell the word, tell yourself this to remember the *i*: *I* am a positive person!

Which animal is the most positive?
The crocodile, because he always looks like he's smiling!

Here's a tip for
SUCCESS today.
Relax! Take a
deep breath and
tell yourself,
"I can do this!"

SUCCESS

word	success
pronunciation	suk-SES
part of speech	noun
definition	the wanted or desired outcome of actions

When something you do is a success, it has come out the way you wanted it to. When you bake a cake and you love how it looks and tastes, that's a success.

  Success is pronounced "suk-SES." There are two tricky *c*'s in the middle of this word. The first *c* makes a "k" sound. The second *c* sounds like an "s." To remember the two *c*'s when you spell this word, keep in mind the following sports cheer: S-U-C-C-E-S-S! That's the way to spell *success*!

"I'm a success today because I had a friend who believed in me and I didn't have the heart to let him down."
—Abraham Lincoln

IT'S EASIER TO

REACH

YOUR GOALS ON

A FULL STOMACH.

REACH

word	reach
pronunciation	reech
part of speech	verb
definition	to stretch in order to get something

Reach is a verb that means "to stretch in order to get something." You can reach with your arm to get something from a shelf, or you can reach with your mind to learn something new.

Reach is pronounced as though it contains two *e*'s: "reech." But that "ee" sound is actually spelled with an E-A combination. To help remember the *a* in *reach*, think of this: If I reach my goal in class, I'll get an A.

"Do not fear mistakes. You will know failure. Continue to reach out."
—Benjamin Franklin

IF YOU DON'T KNOW
HOW TO SOLVE A
PROBLEM TODAY,
BE BRAVE!
ASK YOUR TEACHER
FOR HELP.

BRAVE

word	brave
pronunciation	brayv
part of speech	adjective
definition	able to face difficult or dangerous situations without fear

A brave person can face difficult or scary things without being afraid. Because *brave* describes a feeling, it's an adjective.

You don't have to be loud to be brave. The *e* on the end of the word is silent, but you can't be brave without it!

"We could never learn to be brave and patient, if there were only joy in the world."
—Helen Keller

When you read
a good book, you
can go on an

ADVENTURE

without even leaving

your seat!

ADVENTURE

word   adventure

pronunciation   ad-VEN-chur

part of speech   noun

definition   an exciting and sometimes dangerous experience

An adventure is an exciting experience that can sometimes be dangerous. Traveling to a new country can be an adventure; so can trying a food you have never eaten before.

Adventure contains the word *advent*. An advent is the start of something new. When you begin an adventure, you always start something new.

"I am looking for someone to share in an adventure that I am arranging."
—Gandalf the Grey,
The Hobbit

It's fun to
CULTIVATE
new friendships!
Talk to a new kid,
or maybe join a new
group at lunch.

CULTIVATE

word	cultivate
pronunciation	KUL-tuh-vayt
part of speech	verb
definition	to cause to grow and improve

When you cultivate something, you cause it to grow and improve. You can cultivate a plant by watering it. *Grow* and *raise* are two words that mean the same thing as *cultivate*.

Cultivate has three syllables: cul-ti-vate. Say each syllable slowly to yourself when you spell this word.

"**Cultivate peace and harmony with all.**"
–George Washington

A **FIERCE** male lion can eat up to ninety-five pounds of meat in one sitting. Can you finish every bite of your lunch today?

FIERCE

word	fierce
pronunciation	feers
part of speech	adjective
definition	intensely powerful

Fierce is an adjective that describes something very powerful, strong, or forceful. Fierce things are sometimes thought to be scary.

Remembering the order of the letters *i* and *e* in *fierce* can be tricky, but they follow the common spelling rule: *i* before *e* except after *c*.

What is the best way to talk to a fierce monster?
From far away!

What will you do
for AMUSEMENT
after school
today?

AMUSEMENT

word	amusement
pronunciation	uh-MYOOZ-munt
part of speech	noun
definition	something that is entertaining

An amusement is something that entertains you. Watching a movie is an amusement. So is playing a game. And an amusement park is full of rides and activities to entertain you.

Amusement ends with the letters M-E-N-T, but you might be tempted to spell it with an M-*I*-N-T instead. Think of this sentence to help you remember the correct spelling: To spell amusement, *amuse me*, and then add *nt*.

Why don't mummies like amusement?
They're afraid they'll relax and unwind.

INVEST
your time wisely
today.
Work hard,
but have some
fun, too!

INVEST

word invest

pronunciation in-VEST

part of speech verb

definition to devote (usually time, energy, or money) to a project

When you invest in something, you give your time, energy, or money to it. If you spend the day helping clean up a park, you will invest a lot of good energy! Because you are taking action when you invest, that makes this word a verb.

Here's a way to remember that *invest* begins with the letters I-N: You *invest in* something.

Where do fish invest their money?
In a riverbank!

THE HEAVIEST
SANDWICH IN THE
WORLD WAS MADE OF
CORNED BEEF AND WEIGHED
MORE THAN FIVE THOUSAND
POUNDS. NOW THAT'S A
REMARKABLE
SANDWICH!

REMARKABLE

word   remarkable

pronunciation   ree-MAHR-kuh-bl

part of speech   adjective

definition   unusual and attracting
                        attention

The word *remarkable* describes something that is
unusual and gets your attention. It comes from the
word *remark*, which means "to speak." So when
something is remarkable, you want to tell everyone
about it!

When you're spelling this word, think of a guy
named Mark who is able to do anything!

**Why do so many teachers
use whiteboards?**
They're really re-markable!

Happy birthday!
I can't wait
for the
CELEBRATION.

CELEBRATION

word   celebration

pronunciation   sel-uh-BRAY-shun

part of speech   noun

definition   the act of taking part in a
                       festive event to recognize
                       a holiday, achievement,
                       anniversary, or other happy
                       occasion

A celebration is a fun event to recognize a holiday or
other happy occasion. Parties, festivals, and parades
are all different kinds of celebrations.

You'll notice that the *c* at the start of *celebration*
makes an "s" sound. Use this sentence to help you
remember: I will "c" you at the celebration!

**What kind of cake do elves
and leprechauns like to eat
at birthday celebrations?**
Shortcake!

Even when you
feel alone,
your FAMILY is
always thinking
about you.

FAMILY

word   family

pronunciation   FAM-uh-lee

part of speech   noun

definition   a group of people related to one another

A family is a group of people related to one another. The word *family* can also be used for other things that are related in some way. Apples, oranges, and bananas are all in the fruit family.

   Family ends in *-ly*. These letters combine to sound like "lee." To remember that family ends in *y*, think of all the reasons "y" you love your family!

"*Ohana* means family. Family means nobody gets left behind or forgotten."
—Lilo & Stitch

I KNOW YOU
WILL DO
GREAT
THINGS TODAY!

GREAT

word	great
pronunciation	grayt
part of speech	adjective
definition	considerably better than average or good

Something that is great is better than good—it's outstanding!

Great is an adjective. The letter combination E-A in *great* makes an "a" sound. *Steak* and *break* are other words spelled with E-A that make an "a" sound. So you can enjoy a great steak on your break!

"Some are born great, some achieve greatness, and some have greatness thrust upon them."
—William Shakespeare

It's a
brand-new year!
What GOALS
do you want to set
for yourself?

GOALS

word	goals
pronunciation	gohlz
part of speech	noun (plural)
definition	things set as the desired end results of effort

The word *goals* means "things you decide you want to accomplish before you start something." When you meet your goals, you get the result you wanted. Soccer players can score goals that help them get a desired result: to win a game!

How can you remember the *a* in *goals*? Just think: One of your goals may be to study hard and get an A in class!

"Stay focused, go after your dreams, and keep moving toward your goals."
—LL Cool J

HAVE FUN IN GYM!
WHEN YOUR BODY IS
ACTIVE, YOUR
MIND GETS A
WORKOUT, TOO.

ACTIVE

word	active
pronunciation	AK-tiv
part of speech	adjective
definition	showing a lot of energy

When you are active, you use up a lot of energy!

Active is a tricky word to spell because of its silent *e* at the end. So how can you remember to add it? Easy! You can't spell *active* without an *e* for energy!

An active bull is just called a bull, but what is a sleeping bull called?
A bull-dozer!

ACHIEVE

word	achieve
pronunciation	uh-CHEEV
part of speech	verb
definition	to have success at a high level

When you achieve something, you work hard to succeed at it at a high level. *Accomplish* and *reach* are words that can mean the same thing as *achieve*.

Here's a sentence to help you remember that *achieve* ends in I-E-V-E: *I* hope that *Eve* can achieve her goal.

"**That some achieve great success, is proof to all that others can achieve it as well.**"
—Abraham Lincoln

When you
LEARN
something you don't
want to forget,
write it down.

LEARN

word learn

pronunciation lurn

part of speech verb

definition to gain new information or skills

Learn is a verb that means "to gain new information or skills."

Because it is pronounced "lurn," it can be tricky to remember that there is an E-A combination instead of just an *e* or *u* in the middle of the word. Try this sentence to help you: If you learn to spell *learn* correctly, you'll get an A!

What do elves learn in school?
The *elf*-abet!

It's your
LUCKY day!
I packed your
favorite lunch.

LUCKY

word lucky

pronunciation LUH-kee

part of speech adjective

definition having good luck or fortune

Lucky means "having good luck or fortune." If you are lucky, good things happen by chance and you don't have to do anything to make them happen.

Like many other adjectives, *lucky* is derived from a noun. In this case, we add *-y* to the noun *luck* to make *lucky*.

Some people think seeing a black cat is lucky. When isn't it lucky? When you're a mouse!

Do a MAGIC
trick today.
Make your lunch
disappear!

MAGIC

word	magic
pronunciation	MAJ-ik
part of speech	noun
definition	the power to mysteriously cause events in a way that cannot be explained by nature

Magic is the power to make things happen in a way that can't be explained by nature. A magic trick is not really magic; it's a trick to make you think something magical is happening.

The *g* in *magic* makes a "j" sound: "MAJ-ik." To remember the *g* in *magic*, think of a magician who turns the letter *j* into a *g*!

"You can find magic wherever you look. Sit back and relax, all you need is a book."
—Dr. Seuss

Here's a tip for success:
Before you take a test,

IMAGINE

yourself doing

a great job!

IMAGINE

word   imagine

pronunciation im-AJ-in

part of speech verb

definition   to create an image
in the mind

When you imagine something, you create an image of it in your mind. You can imagine seeing a purple dragon or imagine being ten feet tall.

 Because of how the word sounds, it might be tempting to spell *imagine* with an *a* or an *e* at the beginning. To remember that *imagine* begins with the letter *i*, just think: *I* can imagine great things!

"We do not need magic to change the world. We carry all the power we need inside ourselves already. We have the power to imagine better."
—J. K. Rowling

You have a
TALENT
for making me smile.
Make someone else
smile today, too.

TALENT

word   talent

pronunciation   TAL-unt

part of speech   noun

definition   the ability to do something well

Talent is the ability to do something well. The word *gift* can have the same meaning as *talent*. You might share your gift for singing or dancing at a talent show.

The word *tale* is inside *talent*. Here's a sentence to help you remember: She had a talent for telling a tale.

"Hard work beats talent when talent doesn't work hard."
—Tim Notke

You have been doing
OUTSTANDING
work lately.
Pat yourself on
the back!

OUTSTANDING

word	outstanding
pronunciation	owt-STAN-ding
part of speech	adjective
definition	incredibly good

When something is outstanding, it is incredibly good—and better than other things.

Outstanding can be separated into two parts: *out + standing*. Imagine people standing in a line, and one person standing apart from them. That person is outstanding.

Why did the scarecrow win an award?
Because it was outstanding in its field.

I will always
think you're a
WINNER
if you do
your best.

WINNER

word winner

pronunciation WIN-ur

part of speech noun

definition a successful person

A winner is a person who succeeds at something. A winner can be someone who wins a race or someone who gets an A on a spelling test.

It might be tricky to remember that *winner* has the double letters N-N in the middle. How can you remember the two *n*'s? Think of two letter *n*'s in a race, running side by side. Which one will win?

"A winner is that person who gets up one more time than she is knocked down."
—Mia Hamm

SUPPORT

word	support
pronunciation	suh-PORT
part of speech	verb
definition	to give assistance to

When you support people, you help them. You can support friends by helping them study for a test. You can also support a thing, such as a group, by volunteering.

How can you remember that there are two *p*'s in support? Just think: The two *p*'s in the word support each other!

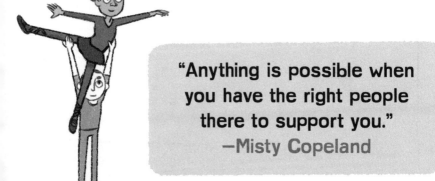

"Anything is possible when you have the right people there to support you."
—Misty Copeland

Here's an
AMAZING fact:
One pencil can
write about
45,000
words!

AMAZING

word	amazing
pronunciation	uh-MAYZ-ing
part of speech	adjective
definition	causing great wonder or surprise

Amazing is an adjective that describes something that causes great wonder or surprise. *Awesome* and *surprising* can mean the same thing.

   To make the word *amazing*, you take the word *amaze*, drop the *e*, and add the ending *-ing*. Remember: If amazing you'll be, you must drop the *e*!

What kind of snake is amazing at math?
An adder!

School is a great place to start a new FRIENDSHIP. Some friends you make now may stick with you for life!

FRIENDSHIP

word	friendship
pronunciation	FREND-ship
part of speech	noun
definition	the relationship between people who know and like each other

A friendship is a relationship between people who like each other. The word *friendship* is a noun, since it's a thing.

To make the word *friendship*, you add *friend* + *ship*. *Friend* can be a tricky word to spell, but remember: A friend is with you to the end, so *friend* ends with the letters E-N-D!

What kind of ship can you find on land as well as at sea?
Friendship!

THIS BRIGHT BANANA

REMINDED ME OF YOUR

BEAMING SMILE.

HOPE IT MAKES YOU

HAPPY TO EAT IT!

BEAMING

word	beaming
pronunciation	BEE-ming
part of speech	adjective
definition	smiling widely with great joy

The word *beaming* describes a smile that is wide and shows great joy. It comes from the word *beam*, which means "to shine brightly."

The letters *e* and *a* in *beaming* work together to make an "ee" sound. It might help you to think of the word *am* in *beaming*: I *am* happy when I see your beaming smile!

"But it is the same soft, lovable face, and the same kind, beaming smile that children could warm their hands at."
—J. M. Barrie

THERE'S A TASTY

TREASURE

IN YOUR LUNCH

TODAY.

TREASURE

word	treasure
pronunciation	TREZH-ur
part of speech	noun
definition	something considered to be important, beloved, or of great value

Treasure is something that is very important, beloved, or of great value. Treasure doesn't always have to be a chest full of gold; your favorite stuffed animal can be a treasure.

Treasure ends with the letters S-U-R-E, which make the word *sure*. To remember that, think of a treasure map. You can be sure you'll find treasure where *X* marks the spot!

> **"There is more treasure in books than in all the pirates' loot on Treasure Island."**
> —Walt Disney

Here's a good habit to DEVELOP: Wash your hands before you eat lunch.

DEVELOP

word   develop

pronunciation   dee-VEL-up

part of speech   verb

definition   to cause to grow

Develop is a verb that means "to grow and become more advanced." Things that develop usually start small and end up bigger or better. For example, a tiny seedling can develop into a full-grown tree.

Some people misspell *develop* by adding an *e* at the end. Just remember: When you spell *develop*, st*op* after the O-P!

What do you give a pig that develops a rash?
Oink-ment!

Lunchtime is a break from your BUSY day. Relax and have some fun with your friends!

BUSY

word	busy
pronunciation	BIZ-ee
part of speech	adjective
definition	doing a large amount of work or activities

The word *busy* means "doing a lot of work or activities."

The letter *s* in *busy* sounds like a "z" when you say the word aloud: "BIZ-ee." One way to remember how to spell this word is that it has the word *bus* inside it. Think of how busy the school bus gets when everyone is on board!

Knock, knock!
Who's there?
Leaf!
Leaf who?
Leaf me alone,
I'm busy!

Your GRADES have been super lately. Good work!

GRADES

word grades

pronunciation graydz

part of speech noun (plural)

definition numbers or letters that show how well a student did on a test or in a class

Grades are numbers or letters that show how well a student did on a test. *Marks* and *scores* are both words that can mean the same as *grades*.

It can be tempting to spell *grades* with a *y* in the middle, like the color gray. Just remember, Y isn't a grade you can receive on a test—and it has no place in the word *grades*!

What grades do pirates get in school?
High C's!

IF YOU DON'T
GET THE RIGHT
ANSWER THE
FIRST TIME,
TRY AGAIN.

TRY

word	try
pronunciation	trahy
part of speech	verb
definition	to do something to see if it works or if you like it

When you try to do something, you do it to see if it works. You might try to fix a broken chair with glue and then realize you need a hammer and nail instead.

Try sounds like the word *why* and other simple words that end in *y*, such as *my*, *fly*, *cry*, and *spy*.

"**Try to be a rainbow in someone's cloud.**"
—Maya Angelou

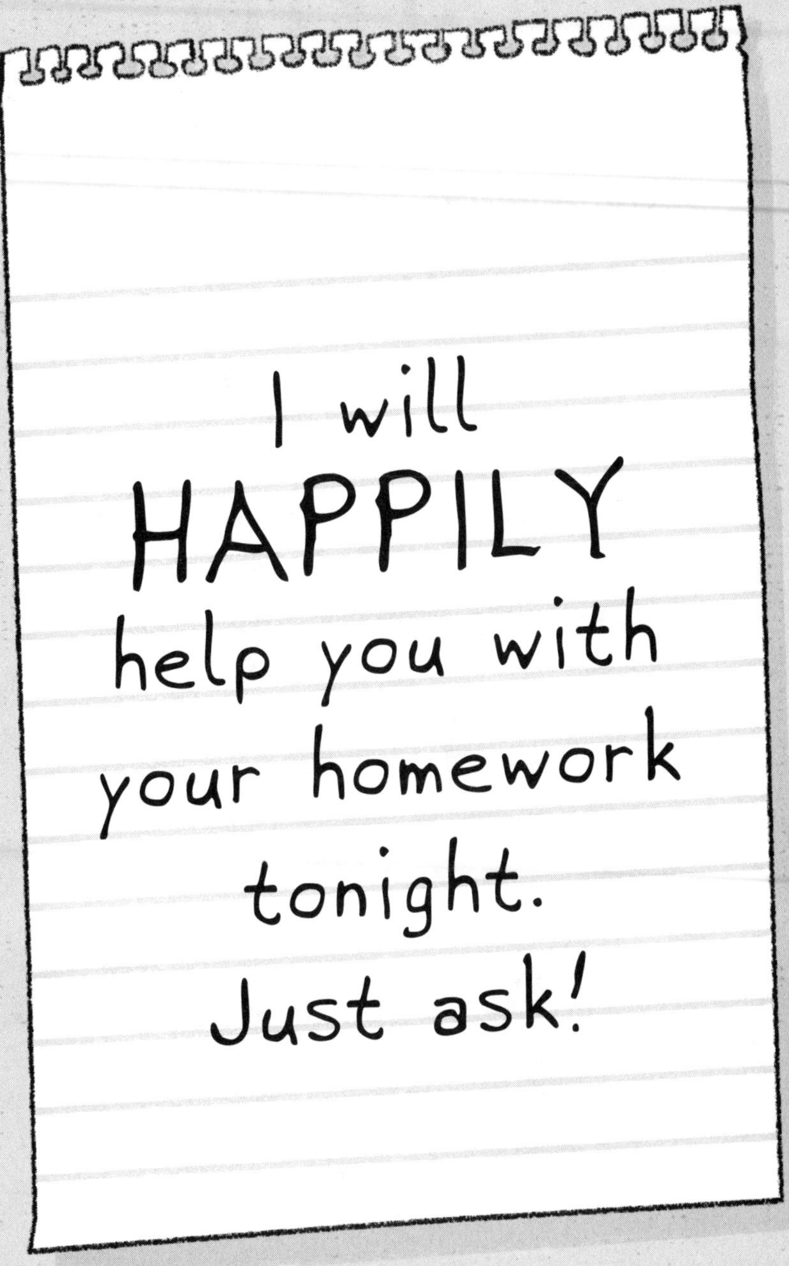
I will
HAPPILY
help you with
your homework
tonight.
Just ask!

HAPPILY

word

happily

pronunciation

HAP-uhl-ee

part of speech

adverb

definition

in a glad or pleased way

When you do something happily, you do it in a happy way. Since it describes a verb, *happily* is an adverb. You can laugh happily, dance happily, or play happily.

To make the word *happily*, start with *happy*, drop the *y*, and add *-ily*.

"And they all lived happily ever after."
—Common fairy-tale ending

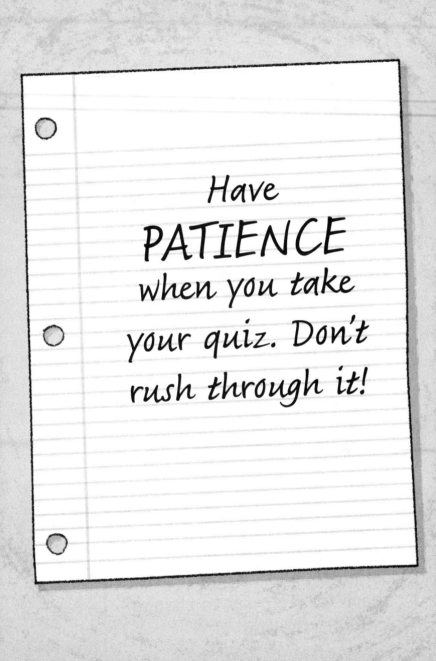

PATIENCE

word
patience

pronunciation
PAY-shunts

part of speech
noun

definition
the ability to accept trouble, inconvenience, or misery without getting upset

When you have patience for something, it means you won't get upset even if that something is difficult or takes a long time to finish.

When said aloud, *patience* sounds the same as the word *patients*, a word that means "people receiving medical care." It is tricky to remember the correct spelling for each word. You will need patience to remember that *patience* ends in C-E.

> "Always remember, you have within you the strength, the patience, and the passion to reach for the stars to change the world."
> —Harriet Tubman

If you find yourself on a team today, COOPERATE! Working together makes teams stronger.

COOPERATE

word	cooperate
pronunciation	koh-AHP-uh-rayt
part of speech	verb
definition	to work with others

Cooperate is a verb that means "to work with others."

The word is made up of two parts: *co* (which means "with") + *operate* (which means "to make something work"). The word is pronounced "koh-AHP-uh-rayt," and you can hear the two different parts of the word when you say it. Say the word out loud when you spell it to remember to include the two *o*'s.

Why wouldn't the triangle cooperate with the circle? Because it thought the circle was pointless!

Be NICE
to others, and
they'll be nice
to you!

NICE

word	nice
pronunciation	nahys
part of speech	adjective
definition	kind and friendly

A nice person is someone who is kind and friendly. *Nice* is an adjective that describes a person. It can also describe things that are pleasant. Cool water on a hot day, for example, can feel nice.

The word *nice* ends in I-C-E. Other words that end the same way are *mice*, *spice*, and *rice*.

"It's **NICE** to be important, but it's more important to be **NICE**."
—Unknown

When you finish
a book, you get a
prize at the end:
KNOWLEDGE!

KNOWLEDGE

word   knowledge

pronunciation   NAH-lij

part of speech   noun

definition   facts and information gained through education

Knowledge is a noun that means "facts and information that you gain through education or experience."

The word *knowledge* is made up of two parts: *know* + *ledge*. *Know* starts with a silent letter *k*, and *ledge* has a silent letter *d* inside it. To remember that *knowledge* contains silent letters, think of a library. A library is a place to get knowledge—and you have to be silent in a library!

Which crawly creature has the most knowledge?
A bookworm!

Keeping your desk
NEAT can help
keep your mind
clear.

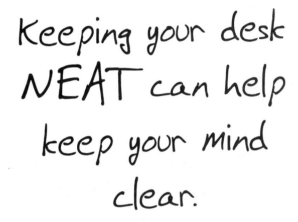

NEAT

word	neat
pronunciation	neet
part of speech	adjective
definition	clean and in order

Neat is an adjective that means "clean and in order." *Messy* and *sloppy* are words that mean the opposite of *neat*.

Neat is pronounced "neet." You can remember how to spell *neat* because it has the word *eat* in it. Think about being neat when you eat!

Why can't leopards ever look neat?
Because they're always covered in spots!

In a few months you will **ADVANCE** to a new grade. But first, enjoy the summer!

ADVANCE

word	advance
pronunciation	ad-VANTS
part of speech	verb
definition	to move forward

When you advance, you move forward. You advance with your body when you run a race. But your body isn't the only thing that can move forward. For example, time advances every second.

The letters A-N-C-E in *advance* sound like "ants." Other words that end with *-ance* and have the same sound are *chance* and *dance*. You can make a sentence with all of these words: You have a chance to advance in the dance contest!

Between lettuce and a tomato, who would be most likely to advance first?
The lettuce, because it's *a head*!

Want to become a spelling star?

Check out this collection of story-based spelling and vocabulary lessons, tips, tricks, and activities designed to give kids a glimpse of the strategies spelling champs use to conquer even the hardest words, developed with the

★ SCRIPPS NATIONAL SPELLING BEE ★

Forty super-short and easily digestible food-themed stories make this the perfect book to share at mealtimes or over the breakfast table (it's more fun than reading the cereal box!), and interactive exercises break down spelling and vocabulary basics in an engaging and accessible way.

For more word-based fun,

spell your way across vibrant U.S. cities, parks, and landmarks in this second collection of super-short, storified spelling and vocabulary lessons, tips, tricks, and trivia facts from the

★ SCRIPPS NATIONAL SPELLING BEE ★

Forty more Bee-vetted and fully-illustrated location-based stories take readers to New York City, Washington, D.C., and beyond, making this the perfect book to share on road trips, buses, trains, and planes—or even at home! Wherever you read it, the takeaway is the same: a mastery of words can really take you places.

About the
★ SCRIPPS NATIONAL SPELLING BEE ★

Each year, millions of students across the country and around the globe come together to compete in classroom and school spelling bees. Of these millions, a fraction will move on to win regional bees and qualify for one of the approximately 280 coveted slots at the Scripps National Spelling Bee, held each May.

Most of the Scripps National Spelling Bee's annual participants are from the United States—but some have come from as far away as Japan, Ghana, and Guam. In order to be eligible to participate in the finals, students can be no more than fifteen years old and can not yet have graduated from the eighth grade. Additionally, previous winners are ineligible to compete again.

You may have seen the finals of the Scripps National Spelling Bee on television or online, but that's just one portion of an entire week of fun planned for the contestants in and around Washington, D.C. During Bee Week, the best spellers in the world come together to celebrate their achievements and make new friends, starting with a big family barbecue packed with great food, field games, dance-offs, and arts and crafts. Every speller is treated like a celebrity—or, as we like to say, a "spellebrity"—and is given an autograph book called the *Bee Keeper* for collecting as many signatures as possible from fellow contestants.

The spellers also have the opportunity to explore Washington, D.C., together and see some of our nation's most historic sites and spectacles. And at the end of the week, there's a formal awards banquet followed by a dance party to give spellers the chance to bid farewell to their 280 new friends.

During the week, contestants regularly have the opportunity to give candid, on-camera interviews with local and national reporters, showing off their love for and mastery of words. This gets them used to the limelight for the competition itself! However, there are multiple rounds of the competition that spellers must tackle before the big nationally televised semifinals and finals.

The competition kicks off with the Preliminaries Test, which consists of both spelling and vocabulary components. Points are awarded for correct answers, and a contestant can earn up to thirty points in this phase of the competition.

Rounds Two and Three follow the Preliminaries Test and consist of oral spelling on stage. Each correct spelling in these rounds is worth three points, and contestants who misspell their words are eliminated from the competition. At the end of Round Three, points are tallied, and up to fifty of the top-scoring spellers move on to the finals.

During the finals, contestants spell words orally on stage, just like in Rounds Two and Three. Any one of the more than 470,000 words in the dictionary is fair game for the competition.

As these finalists go head-to-head on stage for the national title, there are two rules they must keep in mind: they must spell their word within two minutes from when it is first pronounced, and they may not change their spelling at any point. They may, however, ask the official pronouncer for the word's definition, part of speech, language(s) of origin, and alternate pronunciation(s). They can also ask to hear the word in a sentence, and whether they've correctly identified the word's root(s). All of these factors may help a speller determine how to spell a word—and many contestants study other languages in order to make educated guesses about the spelling of unfamiliar words.

Throughout all of this, the stage is surrounded by television cameras for the national broadcast, as well as hundreds of reporters eager to tell the stories of the champions. Everyone is there to cheer the contestants on.

Want to Spell at This Mic Someday?

With some persistence and resourcefulness, it just might happen! All you need to do is become a word collector, just like some kids become toy or rock or coin collectors.

Great additions to your collection are everywhere. For example, if you want to collect food words, flip through your family's cookbooks. Or write down all the new words you see at the grocery store. The produce section and the spice aisle are especially interesting. And restaurant menus are great resources, too—just be sure to check the spelling in the dictionary when you get home.

Read, read, and then read some more. Add to your word collection by looking up and writing down the definitions of words that are new to you.

You can also practice with mini spelling bees at home. Try this: have a friend, family member, or teacher choose a book, magazine, newspaper, or website that you haven't seen, and quiz you on words selected from it randomly. The more you practice spelling, the more confident a speller you will be.

The journey to the Scripps National Spelling Bee starts right where you are: at home or in the classroom, with a list of words and a dream. To learn how to get started in spelling competitions, visit **spellingbee.com** today!